Hi there! I'm Ms. Ashley, a passionate educator, an artist, a proud aunt, and a true NOLA native.

With over fourteen years of teaching experience in New Orleans schools and a Master's in Education, I have now transformed my journey to coaching kids to academic success through my own business –

Ms. Ashley Reading Coach.

I discovered a passion for teaching reading when I began studying the powerful impact of literacy and the joy it brings to individuals. I now create unique and engaging learning sessions, allowing students to grow and thrive in their understanding of the world around them. Coaching others is my passion and purpose. I find immense joy in guiding young learners through the exciting journey of discovering the magic of reading and empowering them to reach their full potential.

This book and resource was created for all little learners and their parents and caregivers to bring literacy development in every household.

TABLE OF CONTENTS

- HOW TO USE THIS BOOK
- COMMON CHALLENGES
- UNDERSTAND YOUR PRE-READER
- HABIT TRACKING
- A - Z LEARNING
- REFLECTION QUESTIONS
- RESOURCES
- READING VOCABULARY

HOW TO USE THIS BOOK

Not sure where to start?
Find the skill your child is working on and jump to that section. There's no need to go in order!

Each concept has three stages: Emerging Pre-Readers, Developing Pre-Readers, and Confident Pre-Readers. Start with any skill and adjust as needed.

Be on the lookout for Parent Tips Boxes throughout the resource for simple ways to keep learning fun and stress-free.

Looking for quick, daily practice?
Keep sessions short, playful, and encouraging—learning to read should feel like an adventure!

Keep it Playful – Learning happens best when kids are having fun! Use movement, songs, and games to bring reading to life.

Follow Their Lead – If your child is fascinated by a certain letter or topic, lean into their excitement!

COMMON CHALLENGES

Letter Reversals (b/d, p/q, etc.)		Many young children mix up similar-looking letters because their visual processing skills are still developing.
Difficulty Blending Sounds		Some kids struggle to smoothly connect sounds into a word (e.g., "c-a-t" into "cat").
Frustration with Tricky Words		Some words don't follow phonics rules (said, was, could), making them harder to decode.
Difficulty Remembering Sight Words		Sight words need to be memorized, and some kids take longer to recognize them automatically.
Trouble with Reading Confidence		If reading feels too hard, kids may shut down or avoid trying.

UNDERSTAND YOUR PRE-READER

Emerging	Easiest

- Beginning to notice letters and sounds
- Enjoys listening to stories and looking at pictures
- May recognize their name or familiar words (like "stop" on a sign)
- Engages in playful "reading" by pretending to read books

What Helps?
- Reading together daily with lots of talking about the pictures
- Singing songs and playing rhyming games
- Making letters part of everyday life (pointing them out on signs, books, or packaging)

Developing	Building Skills

- Recognizes many letters and some sounds
- Begins matching letters to their sounds (e.g., "B says /b/!")
- Can blend simple sounds together in early words (cat, dog, sun)
- Shows interest in trying to "read" on their own

What Helps?
- Encouraging letter-sound connections through fun activities
- Playing simple word-building games (hat → cat → mat)
- Letting them "help" read familiar books by guessing repeated words

Confident	Most Advanced

- Can identify most letters and their sounds
- Reads simple words and recognizes familiar sight words (the, and, is)
- Understands that stories have a beginning, middle, and end
- Starts reading simple books with support

What Helps?
- Practicing early reading with engaging books at their level
- Asking open-ended questions about stories ("What do you think will happen next?")
- Celebrating effort, not just correctness—confidence is key!

Which stage best describes your child? What are they excited about right now?

HABIT TRACKING

READING SKILL	EMERGING	DEVELOPING	CONFIDENT
ALPHABET	○	○	○
BLENDING	○	○	○
COMPREHENSION	○	○	○
DECODING	○	○	○
EARLY READERS	○	○	○
FLUENCY	○	○	○
HIGH FREQ. WORDS	○	○	○
INFERENCE	○	○	○
JOY OF READING	○	○	○
KINESTHETIC LEARNING	○	○	○
LISTENING	○	○	○
MAKING CONNECTIONS	○	○	○
NOUNS	○	○	○

NOTES:
_____
_____
_____
_____

HABIT TRACKING

READING SKILL	EMERGING	DEVELOPING	CONFIDENT
ONSET & RIME	○	○	○
PHONICS	○	○	○
QUESTIONS	○	○	○
RHYMING	○	○	○
SYLLABLES	○	○	○
TRICKY WORDS	○	○	○
UNDERSTANDING	○	○	○
VOWELS	○	○	○
WORD FAMILIES	○	○	○
E**X**PLORATION	○	○	○
YEARNING TO READ	○	○	○
ZEST	○	○	○

NOTES:

LEARNING TO READ ABCs

Aa — Alphabet
Learn the names of the letters in the alphabet

Bb — Blending
Combining letter sounds to form words

Cc — Comprehension
Understanding the meaning of what is read

Dd — Decoding
Identify sounds and blend together to form the word

Ee — Early Readers
Begin to recognize letters, sounds, and simple words

Ff — Fluency
Read smoothly and accurately with expression

Gg — Grammar
Follow the rules that help us construct sentences

Hh — High Frequency Words
Commonly used words to know by sight

Ii — Inference
Use clues to understand what's not directly stated

Jj — Joy of Reading
Encourage a love for books and stories

Kk — Kinesthetic Learning
Move physically to support reading skills

Ll — Listening
Develop Listening Skills for Reading Success

Mm — Making Connections
Linking new words and ideas to what they already know

Nn — Nouns
Words have jobs when they are placed in a sentence

Oo — Onset & Rimes
The initial consonant sound and the end part of a word

Pp — Phonics
The relationship between letters & their sounds

Qq — Questions
Ask & answer questions to improve understanding

Rr — Rhyme
Words that have the same ending sound

Ss — Syllables
Break words into parts, each with a vowel sound

Tt — Tricky Words
Words that don't follow standard phonics rules

Uu — Understanding
Use context and clues to grasp the meaning

Vv — Vocabulary
The range of words a child knows and understands

Ww — Word Families
Groups of words with the same ending

Xx — eXploration
Encourage curiosity & discovery through reading

Yy — Yearning to Read
Cultivate a desire to dive into books and stories

Zz — Zest
Bring enthusiasm and excitement to the reading journey

LEARNING TO READ ABC'S
A GUIDE FOR PARENTS

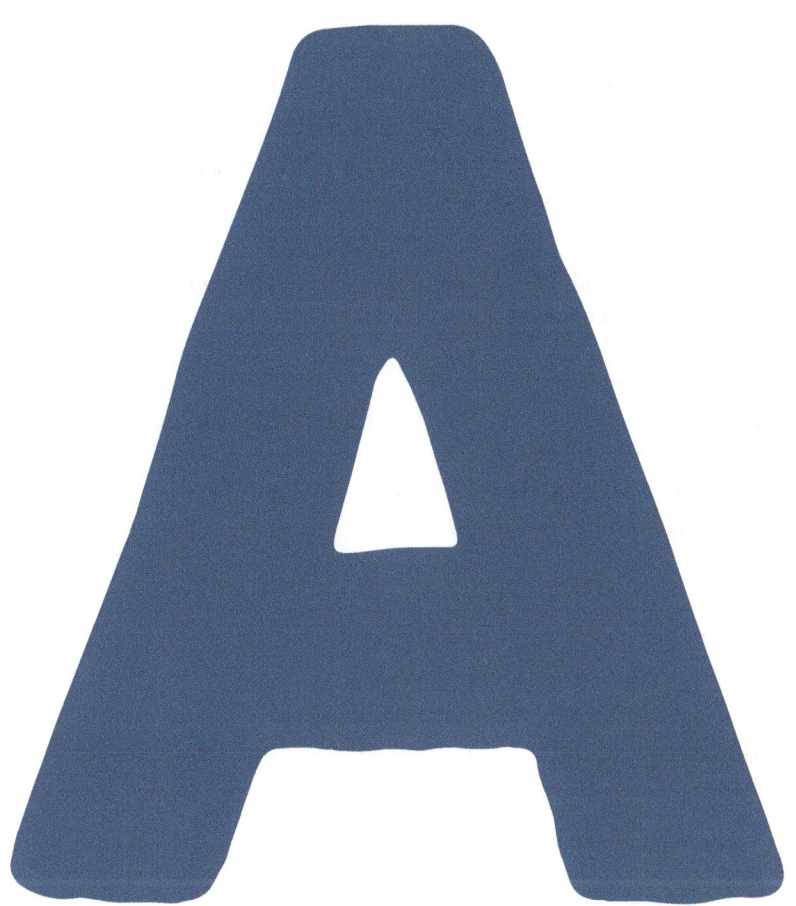

IS FOR ALPHABET

Learning to read starts with the 26 letters of the alphabet—
the foundation of every word your child will ever encounter.

A IS FOR ALPHABET

Emerging	Easiest

Objective: Develop general alphabet awareness and letter recognition
Materials: Alphabet books, alphabet chart/poster

ABC Adventure
- Display an alphabet chart at child's eye level
- Read alphabet books daily, pointing to letters as you read
- Sing the alphabet song slowly while pointing to each letter
- Play "Letter of the Day" - choose one letter to focus on during daily activities

 Make the alphabet visible and part of daily life - your child will naturally begin recognizing letters through repeated exposure

Developing	Building Skills

Objective: Connect letters to sounds and meaningful words
Materials: Letter cards, familiar objects

Sound and See
- Create a simple sorting game with 3-4 letters at a time
- Gather objects that begin with these letters
- Help child match objects to their beginning letters
- Play "I Spy" with letter sounds: "I spy something that starts with /b/" (ball)

 Start with letters in your child's name - they're naturally more interesting to learn

Confident	Most Advanced

Objective: Actively engage with the alphabet through movement and creation
Materials: Paper, art supplies, open space

Moving with Letters
- Create body shapes to represent letters
- Make letter paths on the floor (with tape or chalk) for walking
- Design an alphabet scavenger hunt around the house
- Start a home alphabet book - each page features a letter and beginning sounds

 Let your child lead - if they show interest in certain letters, spend more time exploring those

LEARNING TO READ ABC'S
A GUIDE FOR PARENTS

IS FOR BLENDING

Blending helps kids smoothly connect individual sounds ("c-a-t") to read whole words ("cat"), turning decoding into real reading.

Blending Workbook

 # B IS FOR BLENDING

Emerging	Easiest

Objective: Understand that letters can blend together to make new sounds
Materials: Paper, markers, favorite snack (like chocolate milk for demonstration)

Blending is Like Making Chocolate Milk
- Use a chocolate milk analogy: "Just like blending chocolate into milk makes something new and delicious, letters blend together to make new sounds"
- Start with simple two-letter blends (bl, cl, fl)
- Practice saying the sounds separately, then blend them together
- Draw simple pictures of things that start with these blends (<u>b</u>lue, <u>c</u>lock, <u>f</u>lower)

> 💡 Make the connection physical by letting them stir chocolate milk while learning about blending sounds

Developing	Building Skills

Objective: Practice stretching and blending sounds in simple words
Materials: Letter cards or paper pieces with individual sounds written on them

Sound Puzzle
- Start with Consonant-Vowel-Consonant (CVC) words
- Say each sound separately: "ccc-aaa-ttt"
- Push the sounds together like puzzle pieces
- Gradually speed up until the sounds flow together naturally

> 💡 Use your fingers on the thumb to tap sounds and blend - separate sounds, then bring the sounds together as you blend

Confident	Most Advanced

Objective: Apply blending skills to more complex letter combinations
Materials: Cards with individual sounds, simple word list

Sound Detective
- Introduce three-letter blends (str, spl, spr)
- Play a modified version of your Blending Bingo with simple words first
- Have child listen to separated sounds and "solve the mystery" of what word it makes
- Practice with both reading and speaking the blended sounds

> 💡 Remember some are tricky blends like 'dr' (dragon) - sometimes blends have special sounds that need extra practice

Ms. Ashley Reading Coach @2025

SIMPLE LIST OF BLENDS

bl – black, blue
cl – clock, cloud
fl – flag, flip
gl – glow, glass
pl – play, plate
sl – slide, slip
br – bread, brush
cr – crab, crown
dr – drop, drum
fr – frog, fruit
gr – green, grape
pr – plant, print
tr – tree, train
st – star, stop
sw – swim, swing
sh – ship, shark
ch – chair, chip
th – thumb, thick
wh – whale, when

LEARNING TO READ ABC'S
A GUIDE FOR PARENTS

IS FOR COMPREHENSION

Comprehension helps kids connect words to ideas, emotions, and the bigger picture.

C IS FOR COMPREHENSION

Emerging	Easiest

Objective: Build basic comprehension by connecting pictures to stories
Materials: Picture book, paper, crayons

Be a Story Detective
- Before reading, look at the book's cover and pictures together and predict what might happen in the story
- While looking at pictures, ask "What do you see?" and "What do you think is happening?"

> There are no wrong predictions! Celebrate their creative thinking and help them connect their ideas to what actually happens in the story

Developing	Building Skills

Objective: Connect emotions to story events and characters
Materials: Any favorite storybook

Character Feelings Check
- While reading, pause at key moments
- Ask questions like: "How do you think (character) feels right now?"
- Have your child make face expressions matching the character's emotions
- Connect the story feelings to your child's experiences: "Remember when you felt scared like this character?"

> Help your child build emotional vocabulary by naming specific feelings (frustrated, excited, nervous) rather than just happy or sad

Confident	Most Advanced

Objective: Develop deeper understanding through retelling and personal connections
Materials: Familiar storybook, paper, drawing materials

Story Sharing Time
- Read a story together
- Ask your child to retell the story in their own words
- Draw pictures of beginning, middle, and end
- Make real-life connections: "Has something like this ever happened to you?"
- Discuss what lessons or messages the story might teach us

> Don't correct every detail in their retelling - focus on their understanding of the main ideas and their ability to make meaningful connections

LEARNING TO READ ABC'S
A GUIDE FOR PARENTS

IS FOR DECODING

Decoding is the process of breaking down words into their individual sounds (phonemes) and blending those sounds together to read the word.

D IS FOR DECODING

Emerging	Easiest

Objective: Recognize that words are made up of sounds and letters that work together
Materials: Letter cards, simple books, playdough

Sound It Out Play
- Show a simple three-letter word (CVC like cat) written out
- Say each sound slowly: "/c/ - /a/ - /t/."
- Have your child repeat the sounds while pressing playdough into letter shapes.
- Blend the sounds together to say the whole word.

 If your child struggles, say the first two sounds together first ("/ca/ - /t/") before blending the whole word.

Developing	Building Skills

Objective: Strengthen decoding skills by recognizing letter-sound patterns in words
Materials: Letter tiles, word cards, simple books

Word Builder Fun
- Give your child letter tiles and a set of simple words (bat, hop, sun).
- Say a word and have them build it with tiles.
- Mix up the letters and ask them to rebuild the word by sounding it out.
- Read the word together and find it in a book!

 Use rhyming words (cat, hat, mat) to help children see patterns in decoding.

Confident	Most Advanced

Objective: Apply decoding skills to read short sentences independently
Materials: Simple sentence strips, pointer (like a fun stick or finger puppet)

Read and Point
- Write short sentences on strips: "The cat is big."
- Have your child point to each word while reading.
- If they get stuck, help them break the word into sounds and blend them together.
- Celebrate with a fun "reading dance" when they finish!

 Remind your child that reading is like solving a puzzle—each sound fits together to make words!

LIST OF WORDS TO DECODE

cat
dog
bed
fan
pen
sun
hat
top
tap
log
win
map
fi<u>sh</u>
<u>sh</u>ip
blo<u>ck</u>
plant
drum
swim
bri<u>ck</u>
frog

digraphs =
two letters that make one sound

more complex words with digraphs and blends

LEARNING TO READ ABC'S
A GUIDE FOR PARENTS

IS FOR EARLY READERS

The EARLY READING stage is one of my favorites! Kids are discovering a whole new world, and their brains are eager to soak it all in. At this stage, our goal is to nurture a love for reading.

E IS FOR EARLY READERS

Emerging	Easiest

Objective: Build confidence by recognizing words in familiar settings
Materials: Environmental print (cereal boxes, street signs, favorite snacks)

Word Hunt Around Us
- Point out words on signs, labels, and packages.
- Say, "Look! This says Stop! What sound does it start with?"
- Have your child find letters they know in everyday places.
- Take a "word walk" outside, spotting and reading simple words.

> Use real-life print to show that reading happens everywhere!

Developing	Building Skills

Objective: Strengthen sight word recognition and fluency
Materials: Index cards, markers, simple books

Flashlight Words
- Write common sight words on index cards (the, and, can, play).
- Tape them to the wall and turn off the lights.
- Shine a flashlight on a word and have your child read it.
- Use the words in a simple sentence and read together.

> Sight words are best learned with repetition—keep practicing! The brain thrives on repetition.

Confident	Most Advanced

Objective: Read short books independently and understand simple sentences
Materials: Simple books, finger puppet or pointer

Follow the Finger
- Pick a short book with repetitive text.
- Have your child use their finger (or a puppet) to follow each word while reading.
- If they get stuck, help them sound it out or find a clue in the picture.
- Celebrate when they finish reading on their own!

> Encourage rereading—familiar books help build fluency and confidence!

LEARNING TO READ ABC'S
A GUIDE FOR PARENTS

IS FOR FLUENCY

Fluency is the rhythm of reading. When reading is fluent, it becomes expressing ideas, emotions, and connections.

F IS FOR FLUENCY

Emerging	Easiest

<u>Objective:</u> Develop rhythm and natural flow when reading simple words
<u>Materials:</u> Simple word cards, favorite nursery rhymes

Read with Rhythm
- Clap or tap along while reading simple rhyming words (cat, hat, bat).
- Have your child repeat after you, keeping a steady beat.
- Read favorite nursery rhymes together, emphasizing the rhythm of the words.
- Let them "fill in the blank" for repeated words: Twinkle, twinkle, little ___.

> Singing and rhyming help early readers hear the flow of language!

Developing	Building Skills

<u>Objective:</u> Strengthen reading fluency by grouping words into meaningful phrases
<u>Materials:</u> Fluency phrases, highlighter or colored tape

Phrase Power
- Write a short sentence: The dog runs fast.
- Use a highlighter or tape to mark natural phrase breaks: <u>The dog</u> / <u>runs fast</u>.
- Read it together, pausing slightly at the marks.
- Have your child try reading it smoothly, instead of one word at a time.

> Model fluent reading—read aloud expressively so your child can hear how it sounds!

Confident	Most Advanced

<u>Objective:</u> Read aloud smoothly with expression
<u>Materials:</u> Short books with dialogue, silly voices

Act It Out!
- Pick a book with characters and dialogue ("Let's go!" said Sam.).
- Assign voices—read with a silly, excited, or whispery tone.
- Encourage your child to match their voice to the character's feelings.
- Read the same sentence in different ways—fast, slow, robot voice, grandpa voice.

> Fluency isn't just reading fast—it's reading with meaning and feeling!

FLUENCY PHRASES

The cat sat.

I can hop.

The dog ran.

The sun is hot.

I see a red hat.

Dad can swim.

A big man.

The bag is blue.

The pen is on top.

Can you jump?

The frog hops.

Mom has a cup.

The boy runs fast.

It is a big box.

I see a cat and a dog.

The top is red.

The fish swims.

I see two big rocks.

The bird is in the tree.

The cat and the dog play.

LEARNING TO READ ABC'S
A GUIDE FOR PARENTS

IS FOR GRAMMAR

Grammar is what gives words their job in a sentence—it helps us understand who's doing what, where things happen, and how events unfold.

G IS FOR GRAMMAR

Emerging	Easiest

Objective: Recognize that words have different jobs in a sentence
Materials: Simple sentence strips, color-coded word cards

Word Sort Fun
- Write a simple sentence (The cat runs.) and cut it into word cards.
- Use colors to show different word types (The = blue for articles, cat = red for nouns, runs = green for verbs).
- Mix up the cards and have your child put them back in order.
- Say the sentence together, emphasizing each word's role.

 Start with just nouns and verbs—keep it simple and playful!

Developing	Building Skills

Objective: Identify nouns, verbs, and adjectives in sentences
Materials: Picture books, sticky notes

Find That Word!
- Read a sentence from a book and choose a key word.
- Ask: "Is this a thing (noun), an action (verb), or a describing word (adjective)?"
- Write the word on a sticky note and sort it into the right category.
- Try replacing adjectives with new ones: The big dog → The tiny dog!

 Use everyday conversations—"Can you find a noun in this room?"

Confident	Most Advanced

Objective: Build complete sentences with correct grammar
Materials: Word cards, dice with question words (Who? What? Where?)

Silly Sentence Maker
- Roll a die to pick a question word (Who?).
- Have your child choose a noun, verb, and adjective to make a silly sentence (The purple cat jumps!).
- Write them down and illustrate them for extra fun!

 The sillier the sentence, the more fun grammar becomes!

LEARNING TO READ ABC'S
A GUIDE FOR PARENTS

IS FOR HIGH FREQUENCY WORDS

High-frequency words appear so often, recognizing them instantly helps kids read with ease. Some follow phonics rules, while others need to be memorized.

H IS FOR HIGH FREQ. WORDS

Emerging	Easiest

Objective: Recognize common words by sight
Materials: Flashcards, stickers

Word Sticker Hunt
- Write simple high-frequency words (the, and, is, me) on flashcards.
- Hide them around the room and let your child find them.
- Each time they find a word, they say it aloud.
- Stick a fun sticker on each card as they master the words.

 Keep a few sight words on the fridge or bedroom door for daily practice!

Developing	Building Skills

Objective: Read and use high-frequency words in short sentences
Materials: Magnetic letters or letter tiles, sentence strips, HF Word List

Build-a-Sentence
- Choose a high-frequency word (like).
- Help your child build a simple sentence with it: I like cats.
- Mix up the words and have them put the sentence back in order.
- Read it aloud together, pointing to each word.

 Encourage your child to use high-frequency words in their own spoken sentences!

Confident	Most Advanced

Objective: Read high-frequency words quickly and fluently in books
Materials: Simple books, highlighter strips

Spot & Read
- Pick a book and find a high-frequency word to focus on (said).
- Have your child scan the page and highlight the word each time they see it.
- Read the sentence aloud together, emphasizing the word.
- Try covering the word and having them guess what it is!

 The more exposure, the better—repetition is key with high-frequency words!

HIGH FREQUENCY WORDS

I

a

the

to

and

in

is

it

you

we

he

she

see

can

go

up

down

look

come

here

LEARNING TO READ ABC'S
A GUIDE FOR PARENTS

IS FOR INFERENCE

Inference is filling in gaps and understanding what's not directly stated. Kids become master detectives, finding deeper meanings in every story!

I IS FOR INFERENCE

Emerging	Easiest

<u>Objective:</u> Use picture clues to make guesses about what's happening in a story
<u>Materials:</u> Wordless picture books, storybook with strong illustrations

Picture Clue Detectives
- Look at a picture in a book without reading the words.
- Ask, "What do you think is happening here?"
- Encourage your child to explain their guess using details from the picture.
- Read the text and compare it to their guess.

 Keep a few sight words on the fridge or bedroom door for daily practice!

Developing	Building Skills

<u>Objective:</u> Use story clues and prior knowledge to make inferences
<u>Materials:</u> Storybook, sticky notes

What's Not Said?
- Read a short passage aloud and stop before the story explains everything.
- Ask, "What do you think will happen next?"
- Have your child place a sticky note where they made an inference.
- After reading, check if their inference was correct or if they have a new idea!

 Connect it to real life—"If we see dark clouds, what do you think will happen?"

Confident	Most Advanced

<u>Objective:</u> Infer character feelings and motivations based on story details
<u>Materials:</u> Storybook with emotional moments

How Do They Feel?
- Pause when something important happens in the story.
- Ask, "How do you think the character feels? What makes you think that?"
- Have your child act out the emotion or describe a time they felt the same way.
- Continue reading and see if their inference was correct!

 Inferencing helps kids read between the lines—encourage curiosity and discussion!

LEARNING TO READ ABC'S
A GUIDE FOR PARENTS

IS FOR JOY OF READING

When kids associate joy with learning, they'll keep coming back to books. This passion fuels their growth and makes reading the highlight of their day!

J IS FOR JOY OF READING

Emerging	Easiest

Objective: Create positive reading experiences by making books fun and exciting
Materials: Cozy reading space, favorite books, stuffed animals

Cozy Reading Time
- Set up a special reading spot with pillows, blankets, or stuffed animals.
- Let your child pick any book—even if it's one they've already heard a hundred times!
- Read with silly voices or act out parts of the story together.
- End by asking, "What was your favorite part?"

 The goal is enjoyment—don't worry about perfection or correcting every word!

Developing	Building Skills

Objective: Encourage independence and excitement by giving choices in reading
Materials: Library books, book basket

You Pick, I Pick
- Let your child choose one book to read, then you pick one too.
- Take turns reading—if they aren't reading words yet, have them "read" the pictures.
- Ask, "What do you love about this book?"
- Create a book wish list together for future reading adventures!

 The more kids feel in control of their reading choices, the more they'll love it!

Confident	Most Advanced

Objective: Foster lifelong reading joy by making books part of daily life
Materials: Library card, reading tracker (stickers, chart, or journal)

Reading Adventures
- Visit the library and let your child explore different types of books.
- Start a reading tracker— add a sticker or draw a picture to track
- Encourage them to read to a sibling, pet, or even their favorite stuffed animal.
- Celebrate milestones: "Wow! You've read 10 books this month!"
-

 Joyful reading is about connection—celebrate their love of books in fun and meaningful ways!

LEARNING TO READ ABC'S
A GUIDE FOR PARENTS

IS FOR KINESTHETIC LEARNING

Kinesthetic Learning is a hands-on approach that engages both the body and mind. It's using physical activity and movement to help kids understand new concepts.

K IS FOR KINESTHETIC LEARNING

Emerging	Easiest

Objective: Engage the body in learning letter shapes and sounds
Materials: Sidewalk chalk, playdough, finger paint

Move and Make Letters
- Use sidewalk chalk to draw big letters outside—have your child jump or walk along the shape.
- Roll playdough into letter shapes and say the sounds as you build.
- Finger paint letters on paper while saying each sound aloud.
- Turn letters into movement: "Make a big 'T' with your arms!"

 Kids learn best when they move—don't be afraid to get messy!

Developing	Building Skills

Objective: Strengthen letter-sound connections through movement and touch
Materials: Sand or salt tray, beanbags, letter cards

Feel the Letters
- Pour sand or salt into a shallow tray and trace letters with the finger.
- Toss beanbags onto letter cards—say the letter name and sound before picking it up.
- Clap out syllables in words (el-e-phant = 3 claps!).
- Act out action words (hop, run, spin) while saying them aloud.

 The more senses involved, the deeper the learning sticks!

Confident	Most Advanced

Objective: Apply movement-based learning to reading and spelling
Materials: Jump rope, hopscotch grid, large letter cards

Jump & Read
- Write words on large cards and spread them out.
- Call out a word—have your child jump to it and say it aloud.
- Create a hopscotch grid with words—hop and read as they go!
- Spell words out loud while jumping rope: "J-U-M-P!"

 When reading feels like play, kids stay engaged longer!

LEARNING TO READ ABC'S
A GUIDE FOR PARENTS

IS FOR LISTENING

Children must develop the ability to hear and identify individual sounds (phonemes) in words. They begin to understand how sounds blend together to form words.

L IS FOR LISTENING

Emerging	Easiest

Objective: Develop active listening skills through playful sound activities
Materials: Musical instruments, household objects, listening games

Sound Detective
- Close your eyes and listen to sounds around you—can your child guess what they are?
- Tap a rhythm on a table and have your child copy it.
- Play "I Spy" with sounds: "I hear something that starts with /m/…"
- Read a short rhyme and pause—let your child say the missing word!

 Strong listening skills lay the foundation for phonemic awareness and reading!

Developing	Building Skills

Objective: Strengthen listening comprehension by following directions and retelling
Materials: Simple books, movement-based commands

Listen and Do
- Give fun instructions: "Touch your toes, then hop like a bunny!"
- Read a short story, then ask: "What happened first? What happened next?"
- Pause while reading aloud and ask: "What do you think will happen next?"
- Play "Simon Says": "Simon says find something that rhymes with 'hat.'"

 Active listening helps kids process language and become better readers!

Confident	Most Advanced

Objective: Develop deeper listening skills by making connections to stories
Materials: Audiobooks, storytelling prompts

Listen & Imagine
- Play an audiobook and have your child close their eyes to picture the story.
- After listening, ask: "What did you see in your mind?"
- Tell a story together—start with a sentence, then let them continue.
- Ask: "Have you ever felt like this character? What would you do?"

 Audiobooks and storytelling boost comprehension and imagination!

LEARNING TO READ ABC'S
A GUIDE FOR PARENTS

IS FOR MAKING CONNECTIONS

Making connections helps young readers relate what they already know to the new information they're learning. Whether it's connecting a new word to a picture, remembering a similar word, or linking a story to their own experiences.

M IS FOR MAKING CONNECTIONS

Emerging	Easiest

Objective: Relate stories to personal experiences to build comprehension
Materials: Picture books, family photos

Story-to-Self Match
- Read a picture book and ask: "Have you ever done something like this?"
- Show a family photo and say: "This reminds me of when we went to the park, just like in the story!"
- Have your child draw a picture of themselves doing something similar to the book.
- Use sentence starters: "This story reminds me of when I…"

 Helping kids see themselves in stories makes reading more meaningful!

Developing	Building Skills

Objective: Connect books to real-world experiences and other stories
Materials: Two books with similar themes, nature walk items

Book-to-Book & World Connections
- Read two books with similar themes (e.g., two stories about friendship).
- Ask: "How are these stories alike? How are they different?"
- Go on a nature walk after reading about animals—talk about real vs. story versions.
- Encourage your child to use what they know before reading a book about them.

 Making connections deepens understanding and keeps kids engaged!

Confident	Most Advanced

Objective: Strengthen comprehension by connecting stories to emotions and life lessons
Materials: Storybook, journal or drawing supplies

Life Lesson Link
- Read a book with a strong message (kindness, bravery, teamwork).
- Ask: "What can we learn from this story?"
- Have your child draw or write about a time they learned a similar lesson.
- Discuss how stories can help us understand real-life feelings and choices.

 Encourage reflection—books teach us about life and ourselves!

LEARNING TO READ ABC'S
A GUIDE FOR PARENTS

IS FOR NOUNS

Nouns are the naming words that help kids connect language to the world around them. Learning nouns is a key step in reading because they're often the first words kids recognize, read, and use to express themselves.

N IS FOR NOUNS

Emerging	Easiest

Objective: Recognize that nouns are names for people, places, and things
Materials: Picture cards, favorite toys

Name That Noun!
- Hold up a toy or picture and ask: "What is this?"
- Say: "It's a noun! A noun is a person, place, or thing."
- Sort picture cards into three groups: people, places, and things.
- Go on a "noun hunt" around the house—find and name things in different rooms.

 Turn everyday moments into learning—"Can you spot a noun at the grocery store?"

Developing	Building Skills

Objective: Identify nouns in sentences and everyday speech
Materials: Storybooks, sticky notes

Find the Nouns
- Read a simple sentence: "The dog runs in the park."
- Ask: "What words name a person, place, or thing?"
- Highlight or circle the nouns in a book or sentence.
- Play a "Noun Switch" game— "The banana runs in the park!".

 Encourage your child to describe things with details—more words mean stronger language skills!

Confident	Most Advanced

Objective: Use nouns in sentences to build vocabulary and writing skills
Materials: Word cards, drawing supplies

Silly Noun Stories
- Write three noun categories on separate cards: people, places, and things.
- Have your child pick one from each and make up a sentence.
- Draw a picture of their silly sentence.
- Challenge them to make a short story using at least three nouns!

 The more kids play with language, the more confident they become in reading and writing!

LEARNING TO READ ABC'S
A GUIDE FOR PARENTS

IS FOR ONSET & RIMES

Onset and Rime might sound like teacher lingo, but they're simple and powerful tools for learning to read. Recognizing these patterns helps kids decode, spell, and gain confidence in reading!

O IS FOR ONSET & RIMES

Emerging	Easiest

Objective: Recognize the first sound (onset) and ending chunk (rime) in words
Materials: Letter cards, picture cards

Sound Starters
- Say a simple word like cat.
- Emphasize the first sound (/c/) and the ending chunk (-at).
- Show a picture of a hat and say: "Listen—h-at! It has the same ending as cat!"
- Play a sorting game—group words with the same rime together (bat, sat, mat).

 Rhyme play is an easy way to introduce onset and rime!

Developing	Building Skills

Objective: Blend onsets and rimes to form new words
Materials: Word family cards, magnetic letters

Build-a-Word
- Write a rime (-og) on a card and have your child add different onsets (d-og, l-og, f-og).
- Read the words together, stretching the onset and snapping on the rime.
- Mix up letters and have them rebuild words.
- Try nonsense words too—zog and mog make it silly and fun!

 Play with real and silly words—both help strengthen reading skills!

Confident	Most Advanced

Objective: Use onset and rime knowledge to read and spell unfamiliar words
Materials: Whiteboard, dry-erase marker, word list

Onset & Rime Switch
- Write a word (shop) and erase the onset (sh), asking: "What new word can we make?"
- Swap in a new onset (t-op, m-op, b-op).
- Challenge your child to write or read a new set of words using the same rime.
- Have them read a short story with word families and spot the patterns.

 Recognizing patterns in words builds reading fluency and confidence!

ONSET AND RIME WORDS

b + at = bat

c + at = cat

h + at = hat

m + at = mat

p + at = pat

s + at = sat

b + ug = bug

d + ug = dug

f + ug = fug

h + ug = hug

p + ig = pig

b + ig = big

d + ig = dig

k + it = kit

f + it = fit

s + it = sit

p + ot = pot

h + ot = hot

l + ot = lot

g + ot = got

LEARNING TO READ ABC'S
A GUIDE FOR PARENTS

IS FOR PHONICS

Phonics teaches kids to connect sounds with letters and blend them to read words. Mastering phonics is more than memorizing words—it's learning to read.

P IS FOR PHONICS

Emerging	Easiest

Objective: Recognize that letters represent sounds in words
Materials: Letter cards, objects that start with common sounds

Sound Match Game
- Show a letter card (B).
- Say: "B says /b/ like in ball! Can you find something that starts with /b/?"
- Gather objects and sort them by their beginning sounds.
- Play "I Spy" using letter sounds: "I spy something that starts with /s/..."

 Focus on sounds before letter names—hearing the difference is key!

Developing	Building Skills

Objective: Blend letter sounds together to form words
Materials: Magnetic letters, simple CVC word cards list

Stretch & Blend
- Say each sound in a word slowly: "/c/ - /a/ - /t/."
- Have your child repeat and push the sounds together.
- Build words and swap one letter to make a new word (cat → bat → hat).
- Read short words together, pointing to each sound as they blend.

 Play with real and nonsense words—both build decoding skills!

Confident	Most Advanced

Objective: Apply phonics skills to read and spell new words
Materials: Word list, dry-erase board, simple books

Phonics Detective
- Pick a phonics pattern (sh, th, ch).
- Find words in a book that use the pattern—highlight or write them down.
- Try writing new words with the same pattern.
- Read a short story and use phonics skills to sound out tricky words.

 Encourage your child to use phonics strategies instead of guessing words!

LEARNING TO READ ABC'S
A GUIDE FOR PARENTS

IS FOR QUESTIONS

Questions are powerful tools in learning to read. They help kids connect with stories, think critically, build strong comprehension skills, spark curiosity, and make reading more interactive.

Q IS FOR QUESTIONS

Emerging	Easiest

Objective: Encourage curiosity by asking and answering simple questions about stories
Materials: Picture books, question cards (Who? What? Where?)

Question Hunt
- While looking at a book, ask: "What do you see?"
- Use question cards to guide: "Who is in the story? Where are they?"
- Let your child ask you a question about the story.
- Praise all responses—there are no wrong answers in thinking!

 Asking questions while reading helps kids stay engaged and understand stories better!

Developing	Building Skills

Objective: Strengthen comprehension by answering deeper "why" and "how" questions
Materials: Storybook, sticky notes

Wonder While Reading
- Pause in the story and ask: "Why do you think the character did that?"
- Place sticky notes on pages where your child has a question.
- Encourage them to make predictions: "What do you think will happen next?"
- After reading, go back and discuss their questions—were they right?

 Wondering out loud models how good readers think about stories!

Confident	Most Advanced

Objective: Develop critical thinking by asking and answering their own questions
Materials: Journal or drawing supplies, discussion prompts

Be the Question Master
- After reading, have your child come up with three questions about the story.
- Write or draw their questions and discuss possible answers together.
- Challenge them to ask "what if" questions: "What if the ending was different?"
- Encourage them to explain their thinking: "Why do you think that?"

 Teaching kids to ask their own questions builds deeper thinking and comprehension!

LEARNING TO READ ABC'S
A GUIDE FOR PARENTS

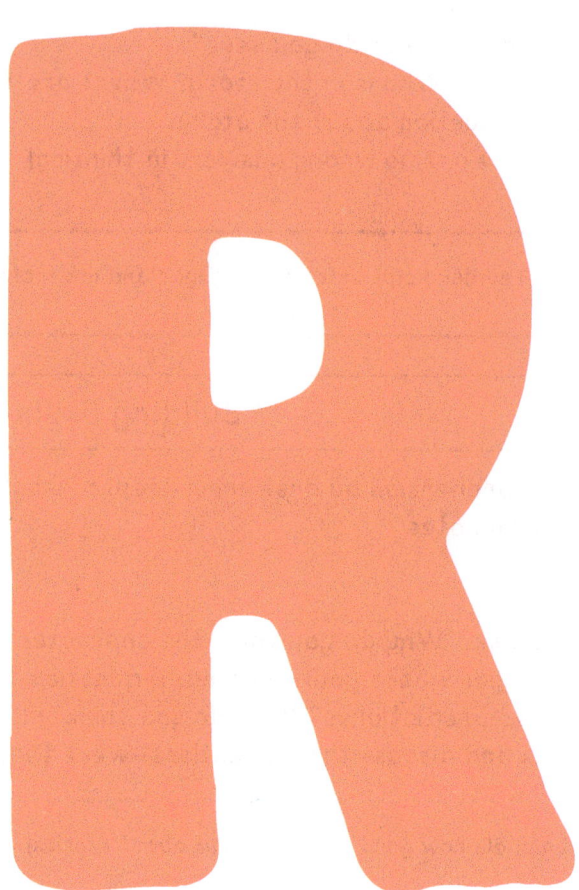

IS FOR RHYME

Rhyming is more than just fun—it's a powerful tool for early reading success! It helps kids recognize sound patterns in words like cat and hat. This strengthens decoding, spelling, listening skills, and vocabulary.

R IS FOR RHYMING

Emerging	Easiest

Objective: Recognize and enjoy words that sound the same at the end
Materials: Rhyming picture cards, favorite nursery rhymes

Rhyme Time Match
- Say two words (cat, hat) and ask: "Do these words rhyme?"
- Show picture cards of rhyming pairs and mix them up—have your child match them.
- Sing nursery rhymes together, emphasizing the rhyming words.
- Make it silly: "Does 'dog' rhyme with 'log' or 'banana'?"

> Playing with rhymes helps kids hear patterns in words, a key pre-reading skill!

Developing	Building Skills

Objective: Generate rhyming words independently
Materials: Rhyming word families (-at, -op, -in), word cards

Finish the Rhyme
- Say a sentence: "The cat sat on the ____." Let your child fill in the blank.
- Give them a word and ask: "What rhymes with 'dog'?" (Real or nonsense words work!)
- Use word families to build new rhyming words: bat, mat, sat, hat.
- Clap out the rhymes to make it more engaging!

> Nonsense words count—wig, zig, blig—it's all about hearing sounds!

Confident	Most Advanced

Objective: Identify and use rhyming patterns in reading and writing
Materials: Simple rhyming books, whiteboard

Write & Rhyme
- Read a rhyming book and have your child listen for patterns.
- Write a word on the board (sun) and list as many rhyming words as possible.
- Create a silly rhyming poem together! ("The cat sat on a hat and found a bat!")
- Have them underline rhyming words in a story.

> Rhyming strengthens spelling skills by teaching predictable word patterns!

LEARNING TO READ ABC'S
A GUIDE FOR PARENTS

IS FOR SYLLABLES

Syllables are like those hidden "clovers" in words. A syllable is like the beat in a word, the heartbeat of language. Once kids learn to hear these patterns, reading becomes more of an adventure.

Syllable Workbook

S IS FOR SYLLABLES

Emerging	Easiest

<u>Objective:</u> Recognize that words are made up of beats (syllables)
<u>Materials:</u> Clapping hands, small drum or table

Clap It Out!
- Say a word (apple) and clap for each part: ap-ple (2 claps).
- Try different words and have your child clap along.
- Use a drum or tap on the table for each beat.
- Sort words by how many beats they have (sun = 1, ba-na-na = 3).

 Start with names—kids love clapping out their own name's syllables!

Developing	Building Skills

<u>Objective:</u> Identify and count syllables in spoken and written words
<u>Materials:</u> Picture cards, jumping spots (pillows, chalk circles)

Hop the Syllables
- Lay out pillows or draw circles with chalk.
- Say a word and have your child jump once for each syllable.
- Show picture cards and say: "How many beats in 'tiger'?" (Ti-ger = 2 jumps).
- Sort pictures into groups by 1, 2, and 3+ syllables.

 Movement makes learning stick—jump, stomp, or tap out syllables!

Confident	Most Advanced

<u>Objective:</u> Use syllables to decode longer words in reading and spelling
<u>Materials:</u> Index cards, whiteboard

Break It Down
- Write a long word (butterfly) and cover part of it.
- Have your child say each syllable separately: but-ter-fly.
- Clap or tap for each syllable, then blend them back together.
- Challenge them to write or think of new multisyllabic words.

 Breaking words into syllables helps with reading fluency and spelling!

LEARNING TO READ ABC'S
A GUIDE FOR PARENTS

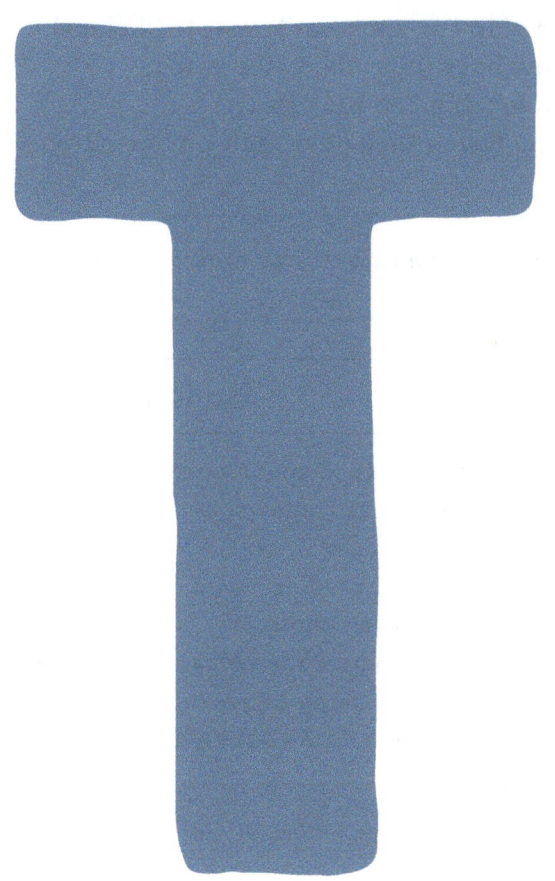

IS FOR TRICKY WORDS

Some words don't follow the usual phonics rules— they can't always be sounded out. Children memorize them through practice and repetition.

T IS FOR TRICKY WORDS

Emerging	Easiest

Objective: Recognize that some words don't follow regular phonics rules
Materials: Flashcards, simple books

Spot the Tricky Word!
- Show common tricky words (the, said, you, was).
- Say: "These words don't sound the way we expect! Let's remember them by sight."
- Read a simple book and point out tricky words together.
- Play "Find the Word" by spotting tricky words on signs or in books.

> Repetition is key—seeing tricky words often helps them stick!

Developing	Building Skills

Objective: Recognize tricky words in context and practice spelling them
Materials: Tricky word list, whiteboard

Say, Spell, Write
- Pick a tricky word and say it together.
- Spell it out loud: "S-A-I-D spells SAID!"
- Write it in the air, on a whiteboard, or with fun materials like sand or shaving cream.
- Read a sentence with the tricky word and underline it.

> Make it multi-sensory—chanting, writing, and reading help kids remember!

Confident	Most Advanced

Objective: Read and write tricky words fluently in sentences
Materials: Sentence strips, index cards

Tricky Word Challenge
- Write a sentence with a missing tricky word ("I ____ playing.").
- Give three-word choices and have your child pick the correct one.
- Write tricky words on index cards—mix them up and have your child read them quickly.
- Encourage them to use tricky words in their own writing.

> Celebrate progress—mastering tricky words makes reading smoother and more fun!

TRICKY WORDS

the

said

you

was

of

where

come

one

have

to

who

does

give

could

their

out

here

put

who

two

LEARNING TO READ ABC'S
A GUIDE FOR PARENTS

IS FOR UNDERSTANDING

True comprehension happens when kids connect words to ideas, experiences, and emotions. With the right support, they'll explore ways to strengthen their understanding!

U IS FOR UNDERSTANDING

Emerging	Easiest

Objective: Build basic story understanding through simple recall
Materials: Picture books, stuffed animals or puppets

Storytime Chat
- Read a short book and ask: "What happened in the story?"
- Use a stuffed animal to "ask" questions like: "Who was in the story? What did they do?"
- Have your child point to pictures and describe what they see.
- Act out a part of the story together!

 Keep questions open-ended—any response means they're thinking about the story!

Developing	Building Skills

Objective: Strengthen comprehension by making sense of events and ideas
Materials: Storybook, drawing supplies

What Happened Next?
- Read a book and pause before a big moment. Ask: "What do you think will happen next?"
- After reading, have your child draw a picture of the beginning, middle, and end.
- Ask: "Why do you think the character did that?"
- Relate the story to their life: "Have you ever felt the same way?"

 Understanding grows when kids connect books to their own experiences!

Confident	Most Advanced

Objective: Develop deeper thinking by discussing themes and lessons
Materials: Books with strong messages, discussion prompts

Big Idea Talk
- After reading, ask: "What was this story really about?"
- Discuss the lesson: "What did the character learn? What can we learn from this story?"
- Encourage your child to retell the story in their own words.
- Have them make up a new ending—how else could the story have gone?

 Talking about books builds lifelong comprehension skills—stories teach us more than just words!

LEARNING TO READ ABC'S
A GUIDE FOR PARENTS

IS FOR VOWELS

Vowels are in every word, making them very important— but they can also be tricky! Their sounds change depending on the word and phonics rules.

V IS FOR VOWELS

Emerging	Easiest

Objective: Recognize vowel sounds in words
Materials: Letter cards, picture cards of short vowel words

Vowel Sound Hunt
- Introduce the vowels: A, E, I, O, U (and sometimes Y!)
- Say a vowel sound and have your child find a picture that matches (/a/ - apple, /o/ - octopus).
- Stretch out words: "C-a-t! What vowel do you hear?"
- Play "I Spy" using vowel sounds: "I spy something with the /e/ sound…"

> Exaggerate vowel sounds—making them silly helps kids hear them better!

Developing	Building Skills

Objective: Identify short vowel sounds in simple words
Materials: Word cards with CVC (consonant-vowel-consonant) words

Sound It Out
- Show a word like cat and say each sound: "/c/ - /a/ - /t/."
- Ask: "What vowel sound do you hear?"
- Swap out beginning and ending sounds (cat → bat → hat).
- Read simple CVC words together, emphasizing the vowel sound.

> Keep it playful—make silly nonsense words to reinforce vowel sounds!

Confident	Most Advanced

Objective: Apply short vowel knowledge to reading and spelling
Materials: Letter tiles, whiteboard

Build-a-Word Challenge
- Say a short vowel word (hop), then have your child build or write it.
- Change one letter at a time: hop → top → tap → tip.
- Have them find short vowel words in a book and underline them.
- Encourage them to write their own short vowel words!

> Mastering short vowels first builds a solid foundation for reading success!

LEARNING TO READ ABC'S
A GUIDE FOR PARENTS

IS FOR WORD FAMILIES

Word families break down the reading process, so kids don't start from scratch with every new word. Once they know a pattern, like -it (sit, hit, lit, bit), they can use it to figure out other words with similar endings.

W IS FOR WORD FAMILIES

Emerging	Easiest

Objective: Recognize patterns in words with the same ending sounds
Materials: Picture cards, simple word family strips (-at, -op, -in)

Rhyme & Match
- Introduce a word family (-at).
- Say: "Cat, hat, bat—they all end the same! They're a word family!"
- Show pictures of words in the same family and have your child match them.
- Sing a word family song: "If you can read cat, you can read hat!"

 Word families help kids see patterns in reading—start with simple, familiar ones!

Developing	Building Skills

Objective: Blend sounds to read and build word family words
Materials: Magnetic letters, word family charts

SBuild-a-Family
- Write a word ending and add different beginning sounds (t-op, h-op, m-op).
- Read each new word together, emphasizing the pattern.
- Use magnetic letters to mix and match new words.
- Read a word family book together (Fat Cat Sat on a Mat!).

 Repetition helps—reading and writing word families builds automatic recognition!

Confident	Most Advanced

Objective: Apply word family knowledge to reading and writing sentences
Materials: Word cards, whiteboard

Write & Rhyme
- Give your child a word family ending (-ig).
- Have them think of and write as many words as they can (big, pig, wig).
- Challenge them to write a silly sentence: "The big pig wore a wig!"
- Read their sentence together and illustrate it!

 Seeing word families in real sentences helps with fluency and confidence!

WORD FAMILIES

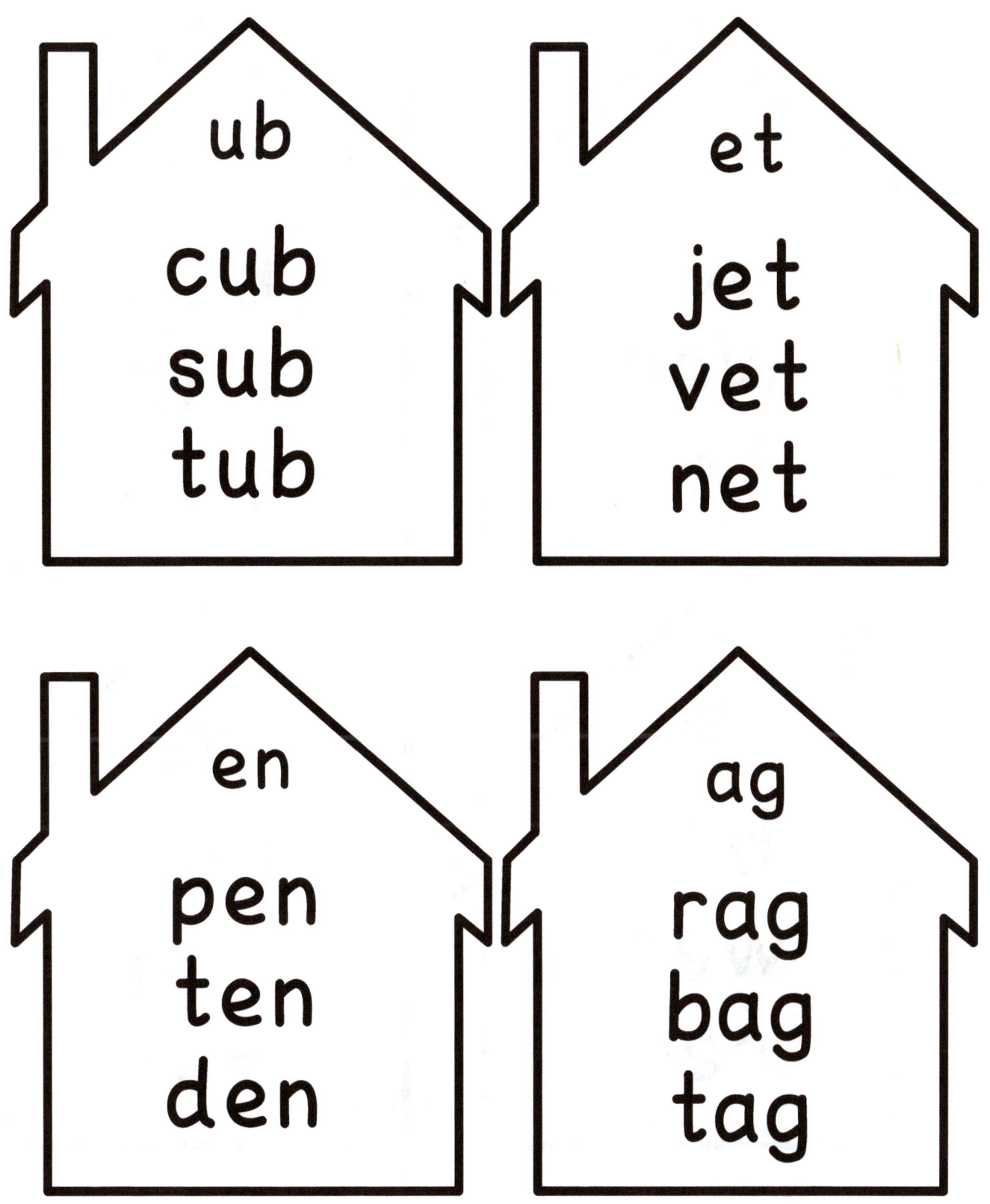

WORD FAMILIES

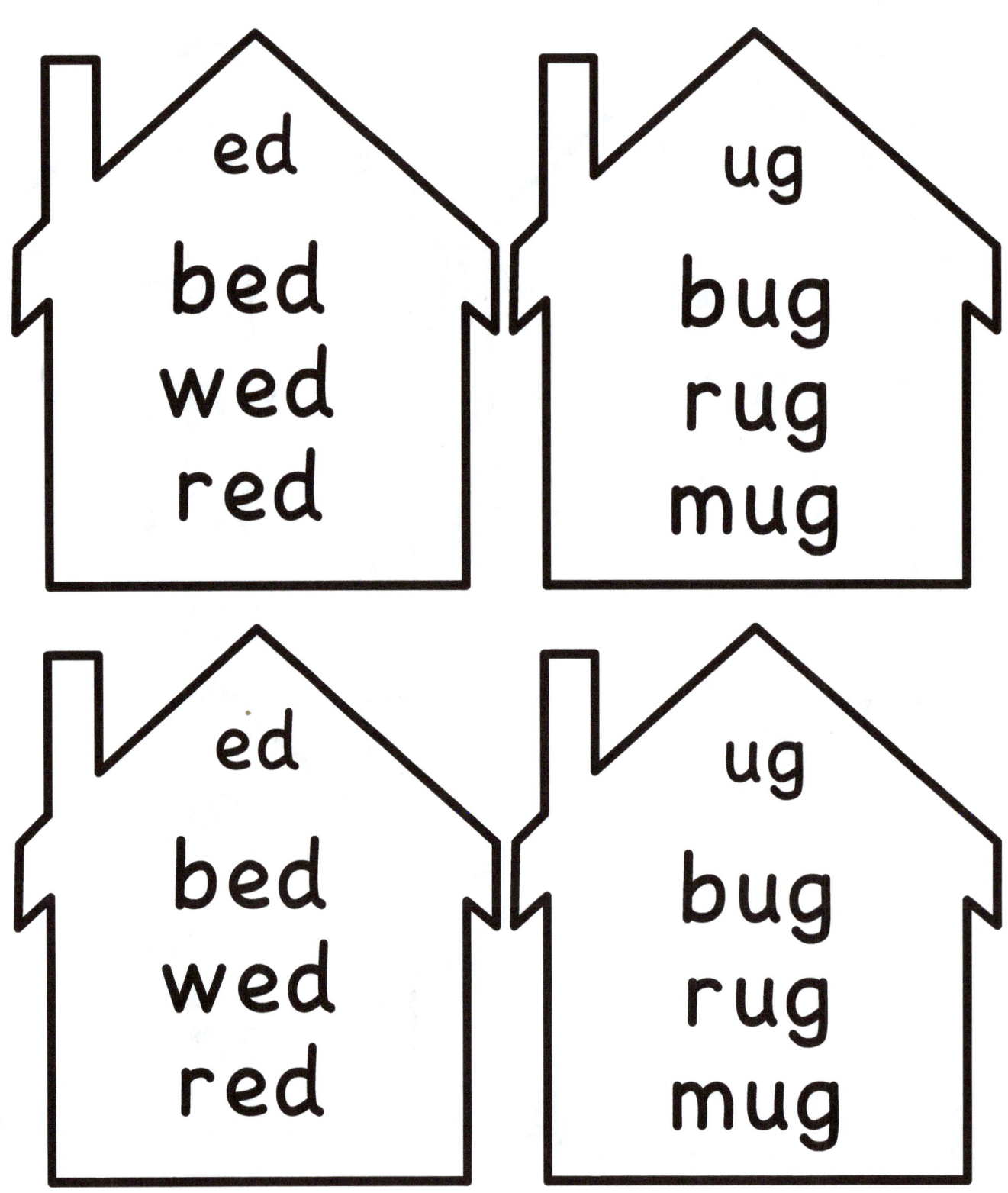

LEARNING TO READ ABC'S
A GUIDE FOR PARENTS

IS FOR EXPLORATION

eXploration in reading is all about diving into new worlds and discovering exciting words and stories. When kids explore different genres, ask questions, they make reading an adventure.

X IS FOR EXPLORATION

Emerging	Easiest

Objective: Encourage curiosity and discovery through books and hands-on learning
Materials: Nature items, sensory bins, picture books

Storytime Adventure
- Read a book about a new topic (space, animals, weather).
- Go on a mini exploration—step outside and find something related.
- Use a sensory bin with objects to match the theme (rocks/dinosaurs, shells/ocean).
- Ask: "What do you want to learn more about?" and follow their curiosity!

 Learning is an adventure—let their interests guide reading choices!

Developing	Building Skills

Objective: Encourage deeper thinking and hands-on discovery tied to books.
Materials: Magnifying glass, nonfiction books, notebook

Be a Word Explorer!
- Read a nonfiction book together.
- Give your child a magnifying glass and let them "search" for new words in the book.
- Write or draw discoveries in an "Explorer's Notebook."
- Ask: "What do you think will happen if…?" and let them experiment!

 Nonfiction books fuel curiosity—pair them with real-world activities!

Confident	Most Advanced

Objective: Explore new ideas through research, creativity, and discussion
Materials: Library books, maps, drawing supplies

Choose Your Own Learning Adventure
- Pick a new topic and gather books about it.
- Read and discuss: "What did you learn? What surprised you?"
- Draw or write about their discoveries.
- Encourage them to "teach" someone else what they explored!

 Exploration builds a love for lifelong learning—follow their questions and see where they lead!

LEARNING TO READ ABC'S
A GUIDE FOR PARENTS

IS FOR YEARNING TO READ

Every child's reading journey is unique—some dive into books eagerly, while others take time to find their spark. The good news? A love for reading can be nurtured!

Y IS YEARNING TO READ

Emerging	Easiest

Objective: Spark excitement and motivation for reading
Materials: Favorite books, cozy reading nook

Book Choice Time
- Let your child pick any book—familiar or new!
- Snuggle up in a cozy reading space.
- Look at the pictures together and talk about what might happen.
- Make it interactive—use silly voices, act out parts, or let them "read" the pictures.

> Giving kids control over their reading choices makes them more eager to read!

Developing	Building Skills

Objective: Encourage independent engagement with books
Materials: Books with repetitive text, bookmarks

Read & Repeat
- Choose a book with a repeating phrase (Brown Bear, Brown Bear, What Do You See?).
- Pause and let your child say the next part.
- Use a bookmark to track progress—celebrate when they finish a book!
- Keep a "To Read" stack and let them pick what's next.

> Familiar books build confidence—rereading is a great way to encourage a love of books!

Confident	Most Advanced

Objective: Foster a lifelong love for reading through meaningful experiences
Materials: Library card, reading journal, special book collection

Reading is an Adventure!
- Visit the library or bookstore to explore new books.
- Start a reading journal where they draw or write about favorite stories.
- Encourage them to read aloud to a sibling, pet, or stuffed animal.
- Celebrate reading milestones ("You've read 10 books this month—amazing!").

> Connect reading to real life—show them that books can teach, entertain, and inspire!

LEARNING TO READ ABC'S
A GUIDE FOR PARENTS

IS FOR ZEST

Zest is the excitement and curiosity that turns reading into an adventure, making every page a journey worth taking. And the best part? It's a skill that can be nurtured!

Z IS FOR ZEST

Emerging	Easiest

Objective: Make reading an exciting and joyful experience
Materials: Favorite books, fun props (puppets, hats, costumes)

Storytime with Zest!
- Pick a lively book and read with big energy—use funny voices and gestures.
- Let your child act out parts of the story with props.
- Pause to ask: "What do you think will happen next?"
- End with a happy dance or cheer: "We love books!"

 When reading is fun and full of excitement, kids will want to do it more!

Developing	Building Skills

Objective: Encourage expressive reading and engagement with books
Materials: Simple books with dialogue, a mirror

Read It with Feeling!
- Choose a book with characters and emotions.
- Have your child read with different expressions—whisper, shout, or make a silly face!
- Use a mirror so they can see how their voice and face match the mood.
- Celebrate enthusiasm: "Wow! That was the best dragon voice ever!"

 Expressive reading builds confidence and makes books come alive!

Confident	Most Advanced

Objective: Cultivate enthusiasm for reading through choice and creativity.
Materials: Book list, blank book for writing their own stories

Create & Celebrate
- Let your child choose a book and share why they love it.
- Encourage them to write or dictate their own mini-book.
- Plan a "Reading Party" where they read to family, pets, or stuffed animals.
- Keep a special book collection of their favorites and add to it over time.

 Passionate readers become lifelong learners—let their excitement lead the way!

REFLECTING QUESTIONS

Learning to read is an adventure, and every child progresses at their own pace. Take a moment to reflect on how your child engaged with the activities.

What Did You Notice? Which activity did they enjoy the most?
_____
_____
_____

Which part felt easy for them? Where did they struggle or need extra support?
_____
_____
_____

Did they show excitement or frustration? How did they respond?
_____
_____
_____

What's one thing you'll try next time to build on their progress?
_____
_____
_____

Are there certain activities or skills they gravitate toward?
_____
_____
_____

Do they prefer movement-based learning, hands-on activities, or quiet reading?
_____
_____
_____

What small successes can you celebrate today?
_____
_____
_____

Every little step forward is progress! Keep reading fun, engaging, and tailored to your child's needs. Celebrate their growth and enjoy the journey together!

SIMPLE WORD LIST

Short A Sound:
Cat, Hat, Bat, Sat, Mat, Rat, Pat, Nap, Map, Cab

Short E Sound:
Bed, Red, Pen, Hen, Jet, Met, Let, Bet, Net, Web

Start with short vowel sound words. These are the first words kids will begin to read and spell.

Short I Sound: Pig, Fig, Big, Dig, Lip, Sit, Bit, Pin, Fin

Short O Sound:
Dog, Log, Pot, Hot, Cot, Lot, Box, Fox, Rock, Sock

Short U Sound:
Cup, Mud, Sun, Bug, Fun, Run, Duck, Bus, Hut, Bun

SIMPLE SENTENCES

- Short Vowel Sounds
- High Frequency Words
- Simple Vocabulary
- Repetition

The cat sat.
I see a dog.
Mom has a hat.
The sun is hot.
Can you hop?
I like red.
The pig is big.
The box is not big.
A rat can run.
The bug is on the mat.
She has a pen.
I am at home.
The bird can fly.
Dad is at work.
We sit on the mat.
The dog is in the sun.
The cat is on the bed.
It is a big fish.
I like to run.
The fox is in the box.

LEARNING TO READ
VOCABULARY REFRESH

DECODABLE BOOKS — These are books that follow specific phonics skills that a child should have previously learned. These skills get more complicated as a level increases.

AUTHENTIC LITERATURE — These books are not following phonetic rules but teaching kids other skills: comprehension, etc. Great as read alouds or even as partner reading.

READ ALOUD — It is highly beneficial for children to be read to. Their brains work so hard with reading and sometimes, they need you to do the work. This is part of development and I use it to model my own thinking skills.

HEART WORDS — Words that do not follow phonetic patterns and students need to recognize automatically, without sounding it out.

HIGH-FREQUENCY WORDS — Words that appear often in a text. These words change as reading levels change.

LEARNING TO READ
VOCABULARY REFRESH

PHONEMIC AWARENESS

The ability to manipulate individual sounds. A foundational skill for reading.
Ex. cat = c-a-t

LETTER-SOUND KNOWLEDGE

Knowing letters sounds is crucial for reading & spelling success. Without knowing letter sounds automatically, students will struggle in all areas of reading.

SYLLABLES

Opening and closing of your mouth around a vowel sound. Every syllable has a vowel.

HANDWRITING

Is knowing how to form letters automatically, without frustration and using the correct pencil grip for proper development.

PENCIL GRIP

One often overlooked but crucial aspect of developing strong reading skills is the development of hand muscles.

www.ingramcontent.com/pod-product-compliance
Lightning Source LLC
Chambersburg PA
CBHW081211170426
43198CB00018B/2919